R's Boat

LISA ROBERTSON

R's Boat

 University of California Press   Berkeley   Los Angeles   London

University of California Press, one of the most distinguished univer-
sity presses in the United States, enriches lives around the world by
advancing scholarship in the humanities, social sciences, and natural
sciences. Its activities are supported by the UC Press Foundation and
by philanthropic contributions from individuals and institutions. For
more information, visit www.ucpress.edu.

University of California Press
Berkeley and Los Angeles, California

University of California Press, Ltd.
London, England

For acknowledgements of previous publication, please see page 84.

Library of Congress Cataloging-in-Publication Data

Robertson, Lisa, 1961–
    R's boat / Lisa Robertson.
        p.   cm. — (New California poetry ; 28)
    ISBN 978-0-520-26239-3 (alk. paper)
    ISBN 978-0-520-26240-9 (pbk. : alk. paper)
I. Title.

PR9199.3.R5316R75   2010
811'.54—dc22   2009037666

Manufactured in the United States of America

19   18   17   16   15   14   13   12   11   10
10   9   8   7   6   5   4   3   2   1

The paper used in this publication meets the minimum requirements
of ANSI/NISO Z39.48–1992 (R 1997) (*Permanence of Paper*).

The ebb and flow of this water, its sound continuous but also marked by motions that ceaselessly patterned my ear and my eyes, supplemented my own emotion, calmed now by reverie, so that I felt in myself, so pleasurably and effortlessly, the sensation of existing without troubling to think.

JEAN-JACQUES ROUSSEAU

We have now reached a stage of experimentation with new collective constructions and new synthesis, and there is no longer any point in combating the values of the old world by a Neo-Dadaist refusal. Whether the values be ideological, artistic, or even financial, the proper thing is to unleash inflation everywhere.

MICHÈLE BERNSTEIN

Contents

FACE/

A man's muteness runs through this riot that is my sentence.

I am concerned here with the face and hands and snout.

All surfaces stream dark circumstance of utterance.

What can I escape?

Am I also trying to return?

Not the private bucket, not the 7,000 griefs in the bucket of each cold

 clammy word.

But just as strongly I willed myself towards this neutrality.

I have not loved enough or worked.

What I want to do here is infiltrate sincerity.

I must speak of what actually happens.

Could it be terrible then?

I find abstraction in monotony, only an object, falling.

Gradually the tree came to speak to me.

I heard two centuries of assonance, and then rhyme.

Had I the choice again, I'd enter whole climates superbly indifferent to abstraction.

I saw amazing systems that immediately buckled.

Here I make delicate reference to the Italian goddess Cardea who shuts what is open and opens what is shut.

I conceived of an organ slightly larger than skin, a structure of inhuman love minus nostalgia or time.

Honeysuckle, elder, moss, followed one another like a sequence of phrases in a sentence, distinct, yet contributing successively to an ambience that for the sake of convenience I will call the present.

I experienced a transitive sensation to the left of my mind.

I am concerned here with the face and hands and snout.

Was I a plunderer then?

I am interested in whatever mobilizes and rescues the body.

I saw the sentiment of my era, then published its correspondence.

I am satisfied with so little.

I felt pampered by the austerity—it pushed my hip so I rolled.

I become the person who walks through the door.

The air goes soft and I'm cushioned as by the skin of an animal.

I can only make a report.

Womanliness knows nothing and laughs.

I can't live for leaves, for grass, for animals.

All surfaces stream dark circumstance of utterance.

I can't say any of these words.

Gradually the tree comes to speak to me.

I collaborated with my boredom.

I write this ornament, yet I had not thought of time.

I come to you for information.

Sometimes I'm just solid with anger and I am certain I will die from it.

I conceived of an organ slightly larger than skin, a structure of inhuman love

minus nostalgia or time.

If only I could achieve frankness.

I could be quiet enough to hear the culverts trickling.

I'm talking about weird morphing catalogues and fugitive glances.

I could have been wrong.

I subsist by these glances.

I desire nothing humble or abridged.

I'm using the words of humans to say what I want to know.

I did not sigh.

I confined my thievery to perishable items.

I do not want to speak partially.

I loosened across landscape.

I doubt that I am original.

I've been lucky and I'm thankful.

I dreamt I lied.

I stole butter and I studied love.

Something delighted me.

And if I am not cherished?

I endlessly close.

But just as strongly I willed myself towards this neutrality.

I enjoyed that pleasure I now inhabit.

I collaborated with my boredom.

I experienced a transitive sensation to the left of my mind.

I stood in the horizontal and vertical cultures of words like a bar in a graph.

I feel like the city itself should confess.

With the guilt that I quietly believe anything, I dreamt I lied.

I felt pampered by the austerity—it pushed my hip so I rolled.

I desire nothing humble or abridged.

I find abstraction in monotony, only an object, falling.

Yet I enjoyed sex in the shortening seasons.

I had at my disposal my feet and my lungs and these slimnesses.

I am satisfied with so little.

I had insisted on my body's joy and little else.

I wish not to judge or to dawdle.

I had no plan but to advance into Saturday.

I had a sense that I'd strengthen, and speak less.

It was a chic ideal.

Look, I'm stupid and desperate and florid with it.

I have a figure of it.

Had I the choice again, I'd enter whole climates superbly indifferent to
abstraction.

I have been like lyric.

I withdrew from all want and all knowledge.

I have myself defined the form and the vulnerability of this empiricism.

I heard that death is the work of vocables towards silence.

I have no complaints.

I could have been wrong.

I have not loved enough or worked.

I have myself defined the form and the vulnerability of this empiricism.

I have nothing to say.

I come to you for information.

I burn, I blurt, I am sure to forget.

In the evening I walked through the terrific solidity of fragrance, not memory.

I heard that death is the work of vocables towards silence.

Honeysuckle, elder, moss, followed one another like a sequence of phrases
   in a sentence, contributing successively to an ambience that for the sake
   of convenience I will call the present.

I heard two centuries of assonance, and then rhyme.

I may have been someone who was doing nothing more than studying the
   Norman flax bloom.

I let myself write these sentences.

I needed history in order to explain myself.

I loosened across landscape.

I raised my voice to say No!

I made my way to London.

I made my way to London.

I must speak of our poverty in the poem.

I can't live for leaves, for grass, for animals.

I must speak of what actually happens—

I'm a popstar and this is how I feel.

I only know one thing: I, who allots her fickle rights.

I feel like the city itself should confess.

I only wanted to live on apples, in a meadow, with quiet.

I can only make a report.

I permit myself to be led to the other room.

I have nothing to say, I burn, I blurt, I am sure to forget.

I preserved solitude as if it were a style.

I am ignorant, but I know.

I raised my voice to say No!

I was almost the absolute master.

I saw amazing systems that immediately buckled.

I enjoyed that pleasure I now inhabit.

I slept like these soft trees.

I'm wondering about the others, the dead I love.

I speak as if to you alone.

Am I also trying to return?

I stood in the horizontal and vertical cultures of words like a bar in a graph.

I can't say any of these words.

I subsist by these glances.

Still I don't know what memory is.

I think of it now as mine.

Here I make delicate reference to the Italian goddess Cardea who shuts

    what is open and opens what is shut.

I took part in large-scale erotic digressions.

The present has miscalculated me.

I want to mention the hammered fastenings in ordinary speech.

I want to mention the hammered fastenings in ordinary speech.

I was willing to suppose that there existed nothing really.

But what I want to do here is infiltrate sincerity.

I was wrong.

I'm for the flickering effect in vernaculars.

I will construct men or women.

I had insisted on my body's joy and little else.

I will not remember, only transcribe.

This is the first time I've really wanted to be accurate.

I will write about time, patience, compromise, weather, breakage.

I sleep like these soft trees in sleep are sweeping me.

I wish not to judge or to dawdle.

I took part in large-scale erotic digressions.

I wished to think about all that was false.

I'm really this classical man.

I withdrew from all want and all knowledge.

In the strange shops and streets I produce this sign of spoken equilibrium.

I write this ornament, yet I had not thought of rhyme.

This is emotional truth.

I'm crying love me more.

Its landscapes are cemeteries.

I'm just a beam of light or something.

I only know one thing: I, who allots her fickle rights.

I'm using the words of humans to say what I want to know.

I did not sigh.

I'm wondering about the others, the dead I love.

I only wanted to live on apples, in a meadow, with quiet.

If only I could achieve frankness.

I had no plan but to advance into Saturday.

In the evening I walked through the terrific solidity of fragrance, not memory.

Life appeared quite close to me.

In the strange shops and streets I produce this sign of spoken equilibrium.

I could be quiet enough to hear the culverts trickling.

In the year of my physical perfection I took everything literally.

Still, the problem was not my problem.

It was the period in which ordinary things became possible.

I am interested in whatever mobilizes and rescues the body.

Life appeared quite close to me.

I will construct men or women.

Limbs, animals, utensils, stars

I crave extension.

Look, I'm stupid and desperate and florid with it.

I do not want to speak partially.

My freedom was abridged.

I speak as if to you alone.

O, to quietly spend money.

I let myself write these sentences.

Of course later I will understand my misconceptions.

I doubt that I am original.

Sometimes I'm just solid with anger.

I have been like lyric.

Still, I don't know what memory is.

I have a chic ideal.

Such is passivity.

I will not remember, only transcribe.

OF MECHANICS
IN ROUSSEAU'S THOUGHT/

The women is itself not a content

It is an unwavering faith in the fictional

Because they don't exist

This work was made under the auspices of opulence

In incandescent occidental forest

In soft pale-green medium-sized notebook

(titled Many Notes Towards an Essay on Girls, Girlhood)

In the coolness descending from trees at night

Mainly I wanted to traverse a failure

Then I wanted the phoneme to spread around me like a sea

I walked beside the absence of

Then one had encountered oneself by leaving

And this posed the basis of a rhythm

As for the theology of certainty

The wrongness is philosophical.

I've spoken about drunkenness, 1975, et cetera

Where the imagined houses the real

What is interesting?

Values are said.

1490, 1501, cosi vulgari, 1503, 1507, 1512, 1513, 1519, 1525, 1539, 1554

With cool specificity of window-light in northern climates

I wanted to make something free

The streets helped me see

How it is that I am soldiered

With political bestiality of each era

I forget it here

Prodigal and Ungrateful

Meet in the speaking likeness

They are observed for rhymes and contiguities

Here the element of time is foreshortened

Rousseau is sobbing out his innocence

By the staggered beds of geranium:

Scripted dissent

Citizen-nerves

Violet stems of thistles

Cement buildings unlit

Odours of hallways

Summer was something pulled out of them

Which, by attraction and radiation

Would embrace and strengthen fiction

To the event of some trees.

How does it feel on your skin?

Slow enough to be accurate

An edge fraying so as to become a chaos

Under full soft hot light

Neither vocabulary at the expense of the other

Here is the concept of a vanishing point

In the form of gold or intense blue

Gently mathematical

I cannot help but penetrate it

To swim in the religiosity of the comprehensible

But the voluptuousness does not appeal to me

Speaking, what was it?

I had a little kettle

I had a habit

I had a sister

A hard time

It was a place like this with several centuries of human death added to it

With small gaps in decorum

And with great opacity

(Even erotic genuflection

Cancelling all that came before)

A hormone is a pierced cell unwinding to the sound of tearing mousseline

The sun has eaten the material

Feminism enters the poem, death enters the poem, rhetoric enters the poem

Out of a sluice of my own making

Then it feels formally false

True and primitive, one at a time

The mouth swings up

With its seven pure, volute resemblances

The little gods are interlocutors

In the mental sensation of living

There are watered meadows in the bodies of thought

Mountains and clouds and paragraphs

Maybe I just needed to presume the freedom of skepticism

And then to immediately part from it

[The jaws speaking

A pebbling sound]

I wanted narrative to be

The proportion in her hair

Not a statement of the type "I am choking"

As an authorizing system

Compared to the encoded unbelievability of women

The river squirts, the thought becomes a chatter

Imitating Pound's Propertius

To make a lack of value

Unseen, unfelt, silent and inflected

And by their fountains

Of hope and demotic ambit

Which glazed, flayed, succulent

Let slip some

Senses

The suppleness of these amusements

Beginning—middle—end

The Etruscan scrotum of clay beneath Perspex

The wrapped breasts of a hermaphrodite

Wished to anticipate

—textile-like—

The padded wall

As loss

The wrongness is philosophical.

October's topmost wandy slim branch

Unsnarls the

Air versus what is

Public: the technology of habit

I awake into an original greediness

Into glossy persimmon-crested notebook called Sylvine

Into large creamy notebook with title Precious Ego

Into small blue-marbled notebook with powder-blue cotton spine

Bought in London, December, 1999

Glossy black notebook with red-ink-edged pages, water dampened

Into many sexes slowly pivoting like leaves

THE PRESENT/

You step from the bus into a sequencing tool that is moist and carries the

    scent of quince

You move among the eight banner-like elements and continue to the edges

    of either an object or a convention

And in Cascadia also

As in the first line of a nursery rhyme

Against cyclic hum of the heating apparatus

You're resinous with falsity

It's autumn

Which might be tent-scented or plank-scented

Their lands and goods, their budgets and gastronomy quicken

You want to enter into the humility of limitations

Coupled with exquisite excess

You walk in the green park at twilight

You read Lucretius to take yourself towards death, through streets and

    markets

In a discontinuous laboratory towards foreignness

You bring his prosody into your mouth

When you hear the sound of paper

C. Bergvall says space is doubt—

What emerges then?

Something cast in aluminum from a one-half-scale model of a freight shed

Intrication

The slight smudge of snow in the shadow of each haycock in the still-green

    field

The hotel of Europe. Its shutters.

Fields and woods oscillate as in Poussin

While the vote is against renewed empire, or at least capital temporarily

Each wants to tell about it but not necessarily in language

I overbled the notational systems in transcription

And my friend was dead

What is the rigour of that beauty we applaud

(Secularly)

At the simple vocal concert?

The otherworldly swan wearing silver and white passes on into current
    worldliness

The steeple-shaped water bottles ranged on the conference table seem
    unconditioned by environments

I had been dreaming of Sol LeWitt and similarity

In somebody's visual universe walking

In the sex of remembering

But I have not made a decision about how to advance into your familiarity

This trade has its mysteries like all the others

It is a labyrinth of intricable questions, unprofitable conventions, incred-
    ible delirium, where men and women dally in the sunshine, their clothes
    already old-fashioned

They can still produce sounds that are beyond their condition

Here is the absurdist tragical farcical twist

In order to enter I needed an identity

In identifying this figure of reversal

The vital and luminous project

Will measure itself against women

And this has seemed poetical

When it is the ordinary catastrophe

I will take the poem backwards to this mistake

I will take your rosy mouth backwards

It is my favourite mistake

This masquerade of transcription

Hands torn crisscrossed

As the medicinal scent rises from books

Like a boat floating above its shadow

Build here the soul of thread

Pluck here the ordinary doubleness

Like delicate men in positions of power

They want the mental idea of the perfect plant

They want the perfect plant also

And I am the person who sits beneath the tree, listening to Calliope,

    attended by luck

Like curiosity translated as society

At 6:30 A.M. it was heavily snowing

The hills not visible, everything blanketed

I watched a pilot boat go out

Into mildness and vowels

Into this great desire to see

Always a boat in the middleground

And in the foreground, the men's powerfully moulded torsos

Twisting and bending persons of the foreground in turmoil

Make livid a philosophy

But not under circumstances of their own choosing

In these persons we glimpse belief

Establishing the fact of perception

Its inherence in history

Now that philosophy is collapsing before our eyes

Our former movements are integrated into a fresh entity, into a freshened
    sensing

And once more I go screaming into sheer manifesto

Also called shape

In several ways, each pigmented and thing-like

In the use of hollow space, which has in it pure transitions

Calm and hostile and alien

In the chirring from the yard

And in the appropriation of falsity

The She is thrown headlong into transcendent things

She swims into splendidness

She bites into her invention and it runs down her face

In this way she is motility

This is different from saying language is volition

Someone stands and weeps in the glass telephone theatre

Someone sits and murmurs

This dog that swims in toxic Latin

Licks his Latin paws

This is the middle of my life

Bringing with me my skin

I go to the library

How will I recognize disorder?

Yesterday I felt knowledge in the afternoon

The alcohol relaxed my body, which made me feel pain

My whole life straddled distance

Who is so delicately silent

By accident, procrastination, debt

I sat in the material tumble of fact in a T-shirt

Say I'm a beautiful animal who has mastered laziness

In reddened clearing in the occidental forest

In the album

Purse of goddess clicking

I long to see how it will continue to behave

And I am walking in her garments

In rooms made of pollen and chance and noise

Towards the errors in humanism

To untwirl that life, puffed and rifled

In the old clothes market

In a tangible humbleness

Smelling of copper and shellac and solder

To the extremity of predication, decay

Among the 804 works, merely to sit in unfamiliar light

In a mauve-toned customized van

Called the Presidential Tiara

Out of belief comes

The yellow light of previous decades in a movie

With flag-iris and wild-rose overhanging

There exists an obsession with structures that dominate position

To produce a deep unease

A hencoop and a kennel

Of high-nosed dogs. Odour

Of sulfur emanating from

A dream of paradise

A CUFF/

It is always the wrong linguistic moment

So how can I speak of sex?

One's own places realism in doubt

But now I want only the discretion of realism

I can't say it any more clearly than this

Philosophers taught me a conversion narrative

How the 4 elements change into each other by flattering

I think of them or meet with them in reading

On Oct. 2 showing their vanity and falsehood

With the frontispiece of him in laurel-crown

The room runs to swags

And popular flower pornography

The house amplifies the trembling as if its inhabitants are lodged in an ear

To make something from what I am

From proximity, bitterness

Is just brutal

So I turned to syllables

And if I degenerate into style

It's because I love it very much

All week long

Like a first thing

Like a technique or a marriage

Where conditions are incomprehensible

Thus satisfying the narrative of the body

Intentionally tawdry and valueless

And this is a recurrent pleasure

Because it gushes it's painterly

So that I feel abstraction

Is an incomplete resistance:

There are explosions of innovation

Next a strange, gilded and embalmed repose

A single leaf laid out the circumstances of its development

So I attended vegetation

Where ornament is always unfinished

And it was a purely melancholic ritual

A fragrance so unexpected emanated from the document

Only to give rise to the striated ruin

Some terrible object presented to it

Dispersed over all the parts

Which are like nature

Miming the human

Painting can be seen as a faltering of that gradient

If faltering begins the ordinary

Discontinuity, seepage and the disobedient will

Sit in the familiar light

Of the person

Without being specifically summoned

The models, the furniture, the clothes are all real

I worked in the kitchen with the windows open

So I could hear you

And change broke my heart

Their hands are love and their faces are love and disturbance

What you see and hear in the present is emotion

We live beyond its limits

The body bandaged to make it more impermeable

Then folded again along the top in a deep cuff

It is 1881, it is Athens, it is Shelley's pyre, it is not his pyre it is his boat, it is
    commodious and utterly dark, it is the camera's movement blocked, it is
    a non-productive economy but it does not deny the socius, it thinks only
    for inconspicuousness, it is only the King, it hardly ever results from
    choice, it masks an entire incompatibility using cloth or cuisine, it needs
    some sort of sacrament or corrosive, it makes its own use of an efface-
    ment, what if it is just angry

If females lick

Language, death, economy

Cold sky with flat grey stormclouds

The seaport at sunset

Tubes of yellow light

This suture is a form of will

Furthermore the paradise is only ever indexical

Above the flat roof of the warehouse called Modern Props

Half-past-five in the afternoon

I'm about to copy this out

Because of having refused to

Break with the tradition of myself

After the recorder is switched on and before I begin to speak

All privacy rubs on it

One's strange bare body needs a party dress

Tyrant body

If it travels

Came into the room as a document

Now these rites have to become intelligible

And wet the shining Babylonian coverlet

It charms impotently like a dialect

Where all the leaves are an opera

Silky things with fringes flung on the furniture

A sort of clown of the feminine

With the head of a nocturnal bird

As an uneven survival

Uneven survival:

Another maudlin dialectic

Billowing skirt over modern corset

By which I am strengthened

With luminous modulation

And outside the window the beautiful socius

In labeled packages

With ship-grey trim

Then with a thorough exploration of those parametres

With instruments made from negation

In the assimilating person

In a pronoun that absorbs everything

We have laid in the vocables of the not-yet-feminine

For a whole sentence at a time I become

The world with its streets, interiors, railroad stations, restaurants, sportscars

    and beaches

If only in some minor respect

Labour was meant to be extricated from these things

The philosophical project of happiness

Approached, pressed against, touched, motionless, in the sun

I wished to pass scrupulously through myself

With subtle stamina

The ceremonies took place

Not to be redeemed

They elaborate one another

A work acts out the severance

There exists a labour towards nothing

Nothing being some kind of sacrament or corrosive

12:30 P.M. Monday

At the beginning of a new series

Just after church bells

I am too slow without you

Neither public nor private but nearly invisible

Seen on a curved stairway from above

Repeated slowly and formally in a dream

Bathers went to and fro through this flower-lined passage

So I pass from institution to intuition

Feeling sad spiritual pressures on the left of my skull

The order seen one night

Lifts, swings onwards in winter light

As for us we are uncertain people

Exploiting mythology in dirty olden sea

To and fro through this flower-lined passage

I slipped across codes

Using rose-thorns

To indicate an idea about embodiedness

By slowing down the causal interval

The idea of the indexical

Is pleasantly estranged, dissolved

In the memory of matter

Such as the beige buildings of anywhere

This is the erotic feeling of non-identity

Suddenly the horizon folds

The biggest problem with melancholy is that it is more detailed than the

world

Now it has spoken in me to become what I will be

Then I would enter the discipline of failure

And at the same time to be disinterested

I think a melting bell is silence

I mean something like this

The world already differs

And astonishment has caused me shame

Whatever listening is to someone

Let it be valued according to its weakness

To annul function

For the size and yield of its fruit

Its surface of variability

And concision and resilience

We manipulate memory

To make things free

I say pricked through, but I also mean

An inflation of monochromy

As a skeptical technique

Which plays out its tensions and conflicts

As in Dürer's *Melancholia*

In a finely textured conundrum

I met with the resistance that

Seeing cleaves

This is to say that labour can move also towards the single blindness I love

What people do is passionate, seen and dominated

Now I feel like I'm that person

Perceiving from a house in progress

To go to the room where life falters

Everything heavy and mortal

Plato, Plutarch, Macrobius, Lactanius and others

Sleep in the capacious singular

I too am cautious

The soul-hormone

Turns the japonica dark

Between stability and volition

Full-blown in the first moments of waking

The action of the sounds comes clear

It's like this—the non-identity of servitude

(The part that makes its own use of an effacement)

Won't ever be revealed

What did radio and the phonograph give

The turn of the phonograph

Could forget about government

All these times and devices

Of significant imprecision

How does the language receive us

It receives us like a surly host

By slow consumptions

Now we run our fingers

Quick and innocuous

In the proper order and sequence and from the beginning

Between the telling and distant objects

Because of my body

In the absence of a system

(It is both in ruins and still under construction)

UTOPIA/

In the Spring of 1979

Some images have meanings, and some have a change in soul, sex or century.

Rain buckles into my mouth.

If pressed to account for strangeness and resistance, I can't.

I'm speaking here for dogs and rusting ducts venting steam into rain.

I wanted to study the ground, the soft ruins of paper and the rusting things.

I discover a tenuous utopia made from steel, wooden chairs, glass, stone,

  metal bed frames, tapestry, bones, prosthetic legs, hair, shirt cuffs, nylon,

  plaster figurines, perfume bottles and keys.

I am confusing art and decay.

Elsewhere, fiction is an activity like walking.

Any girl who reads is already a lost girl.

Women from a flat windswept settlement called Utopia focus on the intricate

  life that exists there.

What I found beautiful slid between.

We die and become architecture.

The season called November addresses speech to us.

The crows are still cutting the sky in half with their freckling eastward wake.

The quiet revolutions of loneliness are a politics.

Some of us love its common and accidental beauty.

I take the spatial problem of heaven seriously.

I look up from my style.

How do people work and sleep?

At about midnight in Autumn

The nightreading girls were thinking by their lamps.

The fleeing was into life.

It was the same world, the same garments, the same loose rain.

It was no longer the end of a season but the beginning.

Clean as a tree, a face waits for form.

At about four in the morning, that first day

Which is a surface?

What is the concept of transformation?

The intellect struggled to its stanza.

The earth spoke in figures.

Its pebbles and tropes and vertebrae withdrew.

I felt a willingness to enter righteous emotion.

I became willing to enter certainty.

Then after a month it was the month of July.

The soft dirt threw the pink light upwards.

The danger of the infinite opened.

It was almost dawn in August.

A dog yipped in sorrow.

By early June, I lost speech.

What about the conceptualized trees?

What about the phosphorescent sexes that took my strength away?

I arrived at the threshold but did not cross.

How odd it is to think that a broken pier laced by gulls and kneeling into

the foaming pull was once an empire.

It is late October.

The house is like sunlight.

Soft and mild emotions were interrupted by emotions that were eager,

   hurrying, impetuous.

People are fragile and finite.

Is this an interesting thing?—to be 40, female, in the year 2001?

How simple it would be to walk together.

It was a Saturday evening.

Yes, the future, which is a sewing motion.

These are the inescapable vernaculars of the Mississauga nocturne.

The effect of the downflowing pattern of shade on the wall was liquid, so

   the wall became a slow fountain in afternoon.

Our fears opened inwards.

Must it be the future?

Yes, the future, which is a sewing motion.

Most decay is not picturesque.

For one day there is the sensation that Springtime is waiting for us to walk

   forward.

Everything follows from the sweet-acrid scent of pencils in June classrooms.

Every angel is fucking the seven arts.

Each leaf had achieved its vastness.

A young woman is seated on a kitchen chair, black wings spread out as if
drying.

It was August and the night was hot.

What we were proposing already exists.

This is a history of sincerity.

The tree uses silence.

The three layers of air flood the sky.

My face is tilted upwards.

I wanted language to be a vulnerable and exact instrument of glass, pres-
sures and chemicals.

It has provided us with a cry but explains nothing.

I understand passivity.

But what elegance is self-sufficient?

Before primrose and before aconite, after snowdrop, at bluebells, during
jonquil, inextinguishably for fritillaria, I stumble in and in.

It began at three o'clock one October afternoon.

What was I to understand of it?

Its intent is mordant.

It's weak and it wants beauty.

It was here that I first observed this question of withheld arcadia.

It leans on the transparent balustrade.

It is a continuous astonishment.

It arrives at nothing but the rolling year.

It always means everything.

For instance, to do, to be, to suffer, to bark, to like, to crumble, to sit: in

each verb I've entertained ambition.

It was only half past eight, but the month was April.

With greeny pleasure I wrote.

This is the melodic contour of the cry of a kind of fruitdove.

People emerged.

My body became apparition in the hot, thin air.

I wrote a story of beginnings, of beginnings, of meat, of words.

I wanted to realize failure as a form of tactile thought.

I intended to be nourished.

Because of the signals communicating from the florescent cavity of the

  chest, because of the vaults of touch, because of the feral knowledge

  moulded by the lips, because of the nearness to armies, because of

  smallness

I intended to be nourished.

And then we went visiting.

It was the Spring of my thirty-fifth year.

Since there was no solitary and free space I made one with my own

  boredom.

I saw that the religiosity of the comprehensible comprised one strand.

Seeing is so inexperienced.

It's not my job to worry about futurity.

I'm on the inside of anything I can imagine.

I wanted to distribute the present, not secure the future.

What could I say that was lasting?

The smell of sex on my fingers was your sex.

Terminological difficulties arose.

That fine day our sunning species was so colourful from the little island to
   which I had swum.

I can but equal them.

It was summer, a hot day.

Who painted the heavy rose?

We devote one of our meetings to love, an elaborate and intact theory.

There are all kinds of experimental protocols.

Tell me if you haven't had grief, a kind of gulped anger or strange freedom.

It could only ever be description.

I would like to enter a bookshop for the coolness and rustle.

I am ordinary and sometimes frightened.

Clouds are really beginning to exist for me.

Always I think I shall save the idea for the future, when I do not.

When will we go to reason?

When did they cease to be rooms?

Twilight is like mercury on queer moss.

The day in the rooms passes.

I noticed the viscosity of dimness.

I felt my arms love.

A man is shouting into a civic silence—please help me, please.

A distant thin ribbon of cirrus ebbs into space.

It was very early in the morning.

Like radios, opiates, the groin's endless currency and surreptitious edge,

   buildings torn out of earth and forgotten

Light could be tasted, had an odour like a tin can.

Girlhood is a landscape.

Across the morning earth, the pangs of a dying economy.

It was 1993.

Yet everything that happened was real, that summer evening.

What's the difference between a behaviour and a game?

The world with its streets, interiors, railroad stations, restaurants, sportscars

   and beaches gains access to surface.

It is not true, it shines from our faces.

In the hinge between these things, a resemblance appears.

I wanted narrative to be a picture of distances ringed in purple.

Then I wanted it to be electronic fields exempt from sentiment.

Then I wanted it to be the patient elaboration of my senses.

Both are mixtures of enigma and proof.

Beneath the culpable excesses, the whole process depended on this same
problem of decay latent within my attention.

An absurdly dominant wakefulness structures the light.

A style creeps up the hills, it is not true either, but it is made from local
materials.

On the second Monday of October, at ten minutes past eleven

I'm referring to the scrim upon which one scribbles the unaccountable, the
pliable and monstrous inner rooms, the solitary shimmer of the video
installation.

I was drunk on well-cut gabardine, jets and failure.

I took literally everything that transpired.

About poverty and ambition:

The account was probably inaccurate.

On a Monday morning in June last summer

Weeds were accurate.

Trees, clouds, faces prognosticate.

These little spiritual boughs of movement hid the lyric.

The sun glitters on the top of the sycamore while the lower branches
deepen to blue.

The sky is the organ of sentiment.

The opacity thickens to topology and backwards to rubbing.

Small foliage brushes the words.

Money is ordinary and truly vernal.

Intensities and climates pass over the face.

Form is not cruel.

I couldn't then reach my thoughts, or recognize the details of my subject:
who the lover was, the distant tile walls of the public transportation
facility.

I'm reminded that Hazlitt spelled browze with a zed.

In late afternoon haze, a fuzz over the distant office towers.

It was its own ruin, that and the ululations of trees.

It was more an undulation than an object, more a gesture than a weight.

It is me.

Life left through the mouth.

Pigment isn't absolute.

Pollen smears the windows.

The blackberry vines are Persian.

The boulder smells faintly of warm sugar.

The core of it fidgets, bleats lustrous polychromes.

The face moves across the human.

Form is not cruel.

The core of it fidgets, bleats lustrous polychromes.

It tastes faintly of warm sugar.

It was more an undulation than an object, more a gesture than a weight.

It was its own ruin, that and the ululations of trees.

It is me.

Gates shut and open.

Also, the tree uses silence.

The next morning, eight o'clock in the morning of June 24th, 1962,

I attempted to picture precisely the scale of my homeplace: low buildings

   squashed or stretched beneath the swallowing sky.

Decay was foreshortened, the element of time removed, so that a building
 standing without walls was simultaneously beginning and ending.

Crisp slithering of dry leaves in August.

Clothes swish through the air.

Books guzzle the distance.

What about the great waxy hoax of the decline of heaven?

Traffic is the puritanical landscape.

Then the figures fall back into anonymity.

The valley ambassadors a largeness.

The thick black rubber lip of the hinged receptacle is the only obscenity.

The shelter of houses groans.

The fountains spurt nectar.

The creek makes a dip.

The contours are amazing.

The century specialized in a style of dress to accent the use of the mind.

The boat moves historically into a form.

So does the pelvis, slung with electrical apparatus.

People moving a one-tonne rose into a truck is communistic.

This year, late in November

People are fucking in the ruins of the recent past.

Mercurial botanies are swiftening.

Masses of women move in the distant street.

I had the body of a woman as far as the hips; below sprang the foreparts of

three dogs; my body ended in two curled fish tails.

I see this from a train.

I wanted to mould verbs from clacking fragments of justice.

Hilarity, spite, and tenderness mingled without quite losing their splendid

morphology.

Here, namelessness is compatible with existence.

Here are pickets, a nut tree.

Girls chat in trees about the mystical value of happiness.

From time to time an "I" appears among the scenery.

Everything is visible, barely disguised.

Clouds float, winds blow, birds fly.

On the left, the remains of a fallen female figure.

A girl stretches up to pick a fruit from a tree.

A city is always a lost city.

A pink city doesn't rise from the forest, but sometimes it does.

Two o'clock, four o'clock

By form I mean the soul of course, that crumpled socket, that splendid
    cosmetic.

Early in 1980

The unstable moving body's making pictures of behaviour.

You will recognize the impenetrable laurel as her home.

The description can't be reproduced.

Someone's history seemed sexy.

Place here a fifty-page description of errors made by the body.

People are flourishing inside all kinds of needs.

Just above a system, the slipping face is flawed and brave for no-one.

It will always be sex for someone who will want it protected as sex.

It only contains space.

It has to do with light, the way light folds on things, the way light folds on
    my point of view.

I was timid in the visual, so I came to utterance—rhythm and subjectivity
   that is.

Into dirt, into earth or whatever.

How do you tread in the world?

A man falls in love with a description of a portrait of a woman.

Whatever girl dares to read just one page is a lost girl, but she can't blame it
   on this book—she was already ruined.

The day shows a licked surface.

Splendid and slow, a waft of dark inwardness surrenders to a system.

There's nothing left to lose.

The day will wrinkle the bare tree, the orange bricks, the slightly different
   birds.

Quietly a shape becomes noticeable.

As I thought about these things, I watched through the train window the
   spongy ground with its buff weeds, the cold neutral sky, the fences of
   gnarled wire and glass, the empty trees with simplicities of branches, the
   coarse pebbly banks or cuts with their soft weeds.

Yet nothing was imitative.

Two o'clock, four o'clock

What still grows in Utopia's deer-fenced garden?

Tansy, thistle, foxglove, broom and grasses shoulder high, some bent plum
   trees persevering, the pear tree chandeliering, geodesic components rust-
   ing in second growth forest.

This is one part of the history of a girl's mind.

The unimaginably moist wind changed the scale of the morning.

Say the mind is not a point of origin, but a skin carrying sensation into the
   midst of objects.

Now it branches and forks and coalesces.

In the centre, the fire pit and log seat, a frieze of salal and foxglove, little
   cadmium berries.

At the periphery of the overgrown clearing, the skeleton of a reading chair
   decaying beneath plastic.

This Is the Beginning of Utopia

Its Material Is Time

PALINODE/

/

Though my object is history, not neutrality
I am prepared to adhere to neither extreme

That which can no longer be assumed in consciousness becomes insolvent
Because it doesn't finish I can be present

So I decide to speak of myself, having witnessed sound go out
Fear is not harmful, but illuminates the mouth

I am not qualified to comment on the origins of the shapes
The archive pivots on a complicity neither denial nor analysis can efface

It is not true, it shines from your face
Against the hot sun that hits us, nothing's peace

And pairs that cannot absorb one another in meaning effects
Go backward and forward and there is no place

This is the border—nothing further must happen
The spurious clacking of grass is a dry spell in thought but not abstract

Just as in dreams there is no limit to further over-determination
I do not wish to enter into that discussion

Memory's not praise or doubt
It is not a substitution, since there is no prior point

There is no limit to its capacity, nothing that it shall not create
I do not in any way wish to escape.

/
It should by no means imitate either the willfulness or the wildness of
nature but should look like a thing
Like free and unfree went walking

To the unseen city of antiquity.

/

Our health was not good
In a particular place I could never use words

If I reason I am not the state's body
Nor is the body someone

It dreams no pronoun
No, not an elevation of any kind, nor any plan

Not even the happy closure
Something, like nothing, happens anywhere

And some never love
Hence they can never be omitted

In their clothing they are not the Kings I know
I realized I hadn't really begun

I seem to have no desires
Or my desire is not very beautiful

Here are new enclosures without end
Perhaps this did not occur in a material sense.

/

The beloved ego in the plummy light is not reasonable
Onwards he coils without touch, and escapes

I do not verify their prognostics
Nothing can be discovered but acts

What will we disappear into if not the moral filigree of praise
Finally nothing but this omnidistant surface

The sense is not the fretful self-important introspection
It was a process of assimilation, not of influence

It follows that these falsified arousals did not motivate memory
But there existed no other theory

How to be happy, how not to die, to lie in bed and think
There is no other priority

Nor could I mint a newer silence
The silence cannot be done into English

There is no choice between historical and hidden meaning; both are present
Presence is not enough

It won't assist my conduct

It was no longer the end of a season
I had no alternative but to become a person.

/
I'm not done with myth yet
A form whose nowhere wrote

Physics is not so much the setting for the fate of the soul, it is the fate of
   the soul
I report my loss to a slightly confused woman not used to the protocol

And I arrive at nothing but the rolling year
The sky hasn't yet reached its full colour

I want to hold belief and dissonance in a cumulative structure that moves
   to no closure
This won't happen because of fear

These techniques are not an end in themselves, nor is continuity
The unseen city of antiquity becomes nothing less than a mediation
   between psyche and history

Not a cloud is to be seen.

/
Nor an orchard nor a single soul nor
A dog nor a leather purse nor subjection

Nor trivialization nor worthlessness
Nor apples nor stars when the festival

Of war unfurls from garden suburbs and
Decks the patios in grand coloured

Swags flipping upwards in the breeze bringing
The shampoo scent of blossoms

It would be nice
To interfere with the accuracy of the world.

/
To try to remember anything about how to exist
In the inchoate institution of

If this is a dress

Nothing but the I am no longer aesthetical trope
As the steeple lightens.

/

To make a mould is a formal gesture of love
There are two ways in which it speaks

Form is not cruel
This by no means suspends the effects of war

I believe that the King remains the West
I'll go into a field with the cattle

To take a rest

At the periphery of the invasions, the fires, the forests
An old man paces.

And if I become unintelligible to myself

Because of having refused to believe

I transcribe a substitution

Like the accidental folds of a scarf.

From these folds I make persons

Perfect marriage of accident and need.

And if I become unintelligible to myself

Because of having refused to need

I transcribe a substitution

To lose the unattainable.

Like the negligent fall of a scarf

Now I occupy the design.

Acknowledgements

Versions of these poems were published in the chapbooks *Rousseau's Boat* (Nomados) and *A Cuff* (Back Room) and in the journals *Chicago Review, Capilano Review, Pilot, Crayon,* and *McSweeney's.* My thanks to the editors.

I am indebted to the Canada Council for the Arts, which supported the writing of this book with a generous grant.

NEW CALIFORNIA POETRY

edited by	Robert Hass
	Calvin Bedient
	Brenda Hillman
	Forrest Gander

Designer *Claudia Smelser*   Text and Display *Garamond Premier Pro*
Compositor *BookMatters, Berkeley*   Printer *Maple-Vail Book Manufacturing Group*

∎